5/24

W9-BMB-964

GETTING TO KNOW
THE U.S. PRESIDENTS

J A M E S K.
POLK

ELEVENTH PRESIDENT
1845 – 1849

WRITTEN AND ILLUSTRATED BY MIKE VENEZIA

CHILDREN'S PRESS®
A DIVISION OF SCHOLASTIC INC.
NEW YORK   TORONTO   LONDON   AUCKLAND   SYDNEY
MEXICO CITY   NEW DELHI   HONG KONG
DANBURY, CONNECTICUT

Reading Consultant: Nanci R. Vargus, Ed.D., Assistant Professor, School of Education, University of Indianapolis

Historical Consultant: Marc J. Selverstone, Ph.D., Assistant Professor, Miller Center of Public Affairs, University of Virginia

Photographs © 2005: Art Resource, NY/National Portrait Gallery, Smithsonian Institution: 24; Corbis Images: 22 (Bettmann), 3 (The Corcoran Gallery of Art); James K. Polk Memorial Association, Columbia, Tennessee: 15 right, 15 left; Library of Congress: 19, 28, 32; Mary Evans Picture Library: 9; Courtesy of North Carolina Historic Sites: 6; North Wind Picture Archives: 12, 27; Steve Wolowina: 26; Stock Montage, Inc./The Newberry Library: 29; University of North Carolina at Chapel Hill/The Graves Family Papers, Southern Historical Collection, Wilson Library: 11.

Colorist for illustrations: Dave Ludwig

Library of Congress Cataloging-in-Publication Data

Venezia, Mike.
  James K. Polk / written and illustrated by Mike Venezia.
    p. cm. — (Getting to know the U.S. presidents)
  Includes bibliographical references and index.
  ISBN 0-516-22616-9 (lib. bdg.)   0-516-27485-6 (pbk.)
  1. Polk, James K. (James Knox), 1795-1849—Juvenile literature. 2.
Presidents—United States—Biography—Juvenile literature. I. Title.
  E417.V46 2004
  973.6'1'092—dc22

                              2004000322

1 2 3 4 5 6 7 8 9 10 R 14 13 12 11 10 09 08 07 06 05

James K. Polk was the eleventh president of the United States. He was born on November 2, 1795, in Mecklenburg County, North Carolina. Although most people today don't know much about James Polk, he was actually a pretty good president.

James Polk did something not many presidents have ever done. He made a list of things he promised to do, and then he actually did them!

President Polk wanted to lower the tariff. A tariff is a tax paid on foreign goods brought into the United States. He also wanted to take the country's money out of different banks and put it into a national treasury so it would be safer. Finally, he wanted to add as much land to the nation as possible. During the four years James Polk was president, the United States grew by about 1,000,000 square miles (2,590,000 square kilometers)!

This is a replica of the log cabin that James lived in until he was ten years old.

When James Polk was ten years old, his family moved from their log-cabin home in North Carolina to Tennessee. James' father became a successful farmer in Tennessee. Even though Samuel Polk owned slaves that worked on his farm, he expected his children to help out, too.

James' brother and sisters all worked very hard on the farm. James did the easier jobs, though. As a young boy, James was sick a lot of the time. Whenever he tried to do a difficult job or play sports, he became exhausted. Sometimes he had terrible stomach pains, too.

By the time James was seventeen, Mr. and Mrs. Polk were quite worried about their son. Finally, Mr. Polk took James to the best frontier doctor he could find. The doctor discovered that James had a serious problem that today would be called bladder stones.

Dr. Ephraim McDowell thought James should have an operation right away. In the early 1800s, operations were extremely dangerous. There were no anesthetics to dull the pain or antiseptics to kill germs. It was a miracle that James got through the operation.

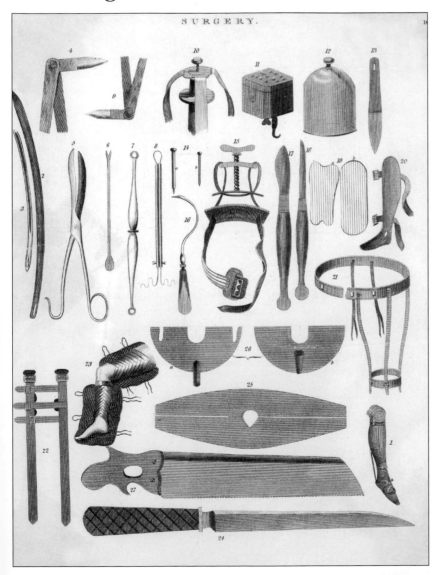

A drawing showing surgery tools used in the early 1800s

Because of his poor health, James Polk got a late start in school. His parents taught him reading, writing, and math at home, but he didn't start regular school until he was about seventeen or eighteen. He must have been the oldest kid in class. James did so well in elementary school, though, that after three years he was able to enter the University of North Carolina as a sophomore.

In college, James was known as an excellent speaker. He became president of the debating team and graduated at the top of his class. During the time he was at the university, James became interested in how state and national governments worked. He decided then that politics might be a good career for him.

The University of North Carolina as it looked in the early 1800s

James thought that the best way to have a successful career in politics would be to become a lawyer. He knew that studying law would help him understand the laws and rules of Tennessee's government. James moved from his home in Columbia to Nashville, the capital of Tennessee. He became an apprentice there to one of the best lawyers in the state, Felix Grundy. James was allowed to study Mr. Grundy's law books and assist him in court cases.

A portrait of Felix Grundy

Mr. Grundy thought James did such a good job that he helped him get a part-time job as a clerk in the state senate. James ran errands and helped keep records. It was a great job for him. He was able to meet important politicians and learn how the government worked.

Even though he worked hard as a clerk, James managed to continue studying. He passed his law exam and became a lawyer in 1820. James left Nashville and headed back to his family's home.

Amazingly, James' first case as a lawyer was to defend his own father. It seems Samuel Polk got into an argument with someone and punched him in the nose!

Portraits of Sarah Childress Polk and James K. Polk

James did a great job in court. Mr. Polk got off having to pay only a one-dollar fine.

While James was setting up his law business, he began dating a girl named Sarah Childress. Sarah was smart and pretty. She also had a great understanding of politics. Sara was the perfect girlfriend for James. In 1824, James and Sarah got married. Sarah was happy to assist her husband throughout his career.

James had begun his political career just before he married Sarah. He ran for a job in the Tennessee state legislature. He worked harder than anyone, traveling day and night to convince voters he was the best person to speak for them as a state representative.

James rode his horse through mud, rain, heat, and dust. He shook hands and talked with anyone who would listen. Because of his determination, James Polk won his first election in 1823.

James Polk served in the Tennessee House of Representatives for two years. During that time, he really impressed people. James was known as someone who would stand up to anyone and vote for what he believed was right, no matter what.

Around this time, James became a loyal supporter of another Tennessee politician. General Andrew Jackson was a popular war hero. When General Jackson decided to run for president, James Polk did everything he could to help him. James liked the way Andrew Jackson cared about solving the problems of everyday working people. He agreed with Andrew Jackson that each state, and not the federal government, should decide for themselves what was best for their citizens.

GEN? ANDREW JACKSON.
THE HERO OF NEW ORLEANS.

   In 1824, Andrew Jackson lost a very close race for president to John Quincy Adams. Jackson's friends were furious. They were bad losers, too, and said John Quincy Adams cheated to win votes.

James Polk was particularly angry. He decided to run for U.S. Congress. That way he could still represent the people of Tennessee while helping Andrew Jackson win the next election. Once again, James Polk campaigned as hard as he could. He was elected to the U.S. House of Representatives in 1825.

Even though a lot of people liked Andrew Jackson, there were almost as many who didn't. Lots of people thought Jackson was a wild, uneducated backwoodsman who would be dangerous for the country. When people criticized Andrew Jackson, James Polk was right there to defend him.

Andrew Jackson finally became president in 1829. He was thankful for all the help James Polk had given him and began doing what he could to help James' political career. In Congress, James even became the leader, or Speaker, of the House of Representatives during a very touchy time.

James Polk served in the House of Representatives (above) for fourteen years.

In the 1830s, most people in the northern states wanted slavery outlawed. Most white people in the southern states wanted slavery to be legal. Sometimes tempers exploded and fistfights broke out. Some members of Congress even brought guns and knives to meetings! James Polk always remained calm, though, and kept things under control most of the time.

After serving in the U.S. House of Representatives for fourteen years, James Polk was elected governor of Tennessee. Then, in 1844, James got the surprise of his life. At the last minute, he was nominated by his friends and supporters to run for president of the United States. James' opponent was Henry Clay, one of the most famous politicians in the country.

A portrait of Henry Clay by Edward Marchant (National Portrait Gallery, Smithsonian Institution, Washington, D.C.)

It was a hard-fought campaign, but in the end, James won by a hair.

One of the first things James Polk wanted to do as president was to add as much land as possible to the United States. Many people in the 1800s felt it was the nation's right and duty to extend its borders all the way west to the Pacific Ocean.

One section of land President Polk was interested in was the Oregon Territory. American settlers had been setting up homes and farms in this beautiful wilderness area for a long time.

The Pacific Northwest became U.S. territory under President Polk.

The United States shared this territory with Great Britain. President Polk worked out a peaceful solution to divide the land up. The United States got what would become Oregon, Washington, Idaho, and parts of Montana and Wyoming. The rest of the land became part of British-owned Canada.

Unfortunately, the next area of land added to the United States wasn't acquired in a peaceful way at all. For years, the United States and Mexico had argued over who had the right to Texas.

By the end of Polk's term as president, United States territory stretched from the Atlantic Ocean to the Pacific Ocean.

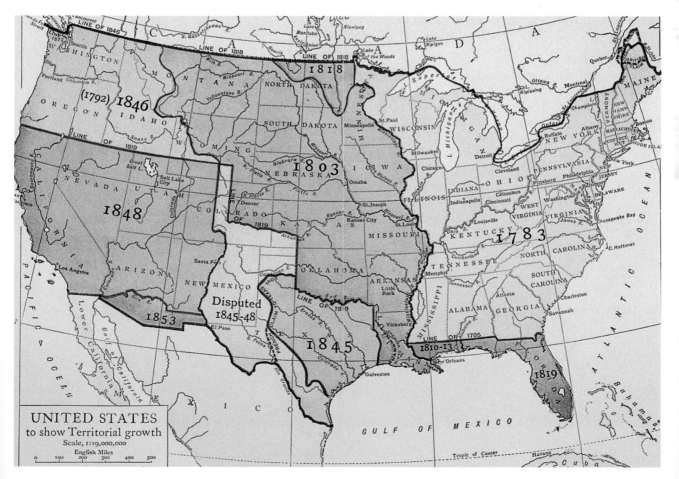

In 1845, Texas finally became a state, but the two countries still disagreed violently over the location of its southern border. It didn't take long for anger to turn into a war.

President Polk chose General Zachary Taylor (on white horse) as one of his military leaders during the Mexican War.

The Mexican War ended soon after U.S. General Winfield Scott captured Mexico City in September 1847.

The Mexican War began in 1846. President Polk chose his favorite generals to lead troops, and he himself made plans on how to fight the war.

After months of bloody battles, the United States won the war in 1847. In 1848, a peace treaty was signed with Mexico. The United States got the border it wanted for Texas. President Polk also gave Mexico $15 million for land that would become the southwestern states of California, New Mexico, Arizona, Utah, Nevada, and parts of Colorado and Wyoming.

President Polk was especially happy about acquiring California. With that region's important seaport harbors, the president felt that the nation was now complete. Its territory stretched from the Atlantic Ocean to the Pacific Ocean.

A photograph of James K. Polk as an older man

Aside from expanding the American frontier, James Polk set up a treasury system to protect the country's money. He also lowered the tax on foreign goods brought into the United States. Some people, though, felt that President Polk never did enough to solve the nation's most serious problem, slavery.

James Polk left the presidency after serving one four-year term. Unfortunately, he wasn't able to enjoy a long retirement. James K. Polk died on June 15, 1849, three months after he left the White House.